Original title:
You Can Do This

Author: Samira Siil
ISBN HARDBACK: 978-9916-87-038-9
ISBN PAPERBACK: 978-9916-87-039-6

Beyond the Stars

In the hush of the night sky,
Dreams take flight on silver wings.
Whispers of the cosmos sigh,
Telling tales that starlight brings.

Planets dance in a silent waltz,
Nebulae glow with colors bright.
Timeless wonders with no faults,
Illuminate the velvet night.

From earth we gaze with hopeful eyes,
Yearning for what lies out there.
Galaxies spin, a grand surprise,
Infinity caught in a stare.

In the heart of the dark expanse,
Mysteries beckon, calling near.
Every twinkle crowns the chance,
To dream beyond what we hold dear.

So let us reach with outstretched hands,
For the stars that shine above.
In that endless space, it spans,
Awakens every soul with love.

Unfurl Your Dreams

Beneath the stars, let wishes soar,
Each hope a wave upon the shore.
Embrace the dawn, let spirits rise,
For dreams are whispers in the skies.

With open hearts, we chase the light,
Through shadows cast, we find our sight.
Unfurl your dreams, let courage bloom,
In every heart, dispel the gloom.

Each step we take, a path we pave,
With passion's fire, we learn to brave.
Together bound, we're never lost,
For every dream, we count the cost.

Forge Your Path

In a world of stone and clay,
Shape your dreams, find your way.
With each step that you take,
Build the life you wish to make.

Through the valleys, through the peaks,
Listen close, the silence speaks.
Carve your name upon the land,
Stand up tall, make your stand.

When the shadows dim the light,
Let your heart guide through the night.
In the forge, your spirit's fire,
Ignite the strength, reach higher.

Let the challenges unfold,
In your hands, the future’s gold.
With courage, face what’s unknown,
Forge ahead, you are not alone.

Every stumble, every fall,
Rising stronger, hear the call.
You are the master of your fate,
Now’s the time, don’t hesitate.

A Canvas of Hope

Upon this canvas, colors blend,
With every stroke, new tales we send.
In hues of peace, we paint our days,
Creating light in countless ways.

Bold lines of joy, soft strokes of love,
In this vast world, we're all a part.
From darkness springs a vibrant theme,
Life's masterpiece, a living dream.

Through every trial, the brush we wield,
In hands of hope, our fate is sealed.
With every heartbeat, art unfolds,
A testament to dreams retold.

Beyond the Horizon

Waves crash gently on the shore,
Whispers calling, hearts want more.
Beyond the horizon, dreams await,
Embrace the journey, don’t hesitate.

Mountains rise with peaks so grand,
Nature holds our hopes in hand.
With every step upon this quest,
We’ll find the path that leads to rest.

Stars will guide us through the night,
Every doubt fades with their light.
Far beyond the limits known,
We'll carve a place that feels like home.

Adventures call, we’ll take the chance,
In every heartbeat, there’s a dance.
Life's a canvas, paint it wide,
Beyond the horizon, dreams abide.

Relentless Pursuit

In the race of life, we forge ahead,
With dreams as fuel, no fear to shed.
Through winding paths, our spirits shine,
In relentless pursuit, hearts intertwine.

Each challenge faced, a chance to grow,
In every setback, a seed to sow.
With every step, our vision clear,
For in our hearts, we hold what's dear.

Together we stand, through thick and thin,
With courage fierce, we rise again.
In pursuit of greatness, we won't relent,
With passion burning, our souls are lent.

Rise and Shine

Morning breaks with light so bright,
Hope awakens in the sight.
Birds are singing, skies are clear,
A brand new day is finally here.

Take a breath, feel the breeze,
Nature whispers through the trees.
Every moment speaks so true,
Shine your light and just break through.

Clouds drift by, no need to fear,
Embrace the warmth that draws you near.
With each step, let courage rise,
Chase your dreams and touch the skies.

As the sun begins to climb,
Feel the rhythm, keep the time.
Life’s a dance, so join the play,
Rise and shine, seize the day!

Unyielding Spirit

In the face of strife we stand,
Fists held high, we lend a hand.
Through the storms and trials faced,
Our spirit strong, no time to waste.

Beneath the weight, we do not bend,
A bond like ours will never end.
With hearts of fire, we carry on,
In every dusk, we greet the dawn.

Through the shadows, we will fight,
With courage blazing, fierce and bright.
For dreams ignite the darkest night,
Together, we shall find the light.

Unyielding hearts in every fight,
We rise again, our hopes in sight.
With every challenge, we grow strong,
In unity, we all belong.

Wings of Determination

In the sky, a bird takes flight,
Soaring high with pure delight.
Wings unfurl with grace and speed,
On the winds, we plant the seed.

Challenges may come our way,
But with each trial, we won't sway.
With every glance towards the sun,
We hold the strength of everyone.

No fear of heights, we aim to rise,
Chasing dreams that touch the skies.
With hearts ablaze, we forge ahead,
Wings of fire under our spread.

With every beat, our spirits soar,
Determined souls that yearn for more.
Together strong, we’ll stake our claim,
With wings of courage, we’ll stake our name.

The Power to Prevail

In shadows deep, we find our light,
With faith as strong, we rise from night.
Each challenge faced, a step we take,
United hearts, for hope's sweet sake.

Through storms we soar, with wings of grace,
Embracing change, we find our place.
Resilience born from trials faced,
In every struggle, strength is traced.

We stand as one, unyielding force,
With courage guiding our true course.
In every tear, a lesson learned,
For in the fire, our hearts have burned.

Embrace the Climb

Each mountain holds a tale untold,
With peaks of silver, cliffs of gold.
Take a breath, lift your gaze,
Embrace the climb in all its ways.

Through the fog and through the pain,
Find the joy in every gain.
Step by step, you're not confined,
In the journey, strength you'll find.

Let the wind whisper to your soul,
Feel the thrill, it's time to roll.
With every struggle, every fight,
You grow bolder, shine so bright.

As the summit comes to view,
Know the climb has molded you.
With open hearts, take a chance,
Celebrate this warrior's dance.

Embrace the climb, it's yours to take,
With steadfast will, your heart won’t break.
For in each rise, there’s love and light,
Keep on climbing, reach new heights.

Heart of a Warrior

In the shadows where fears dwell,
A warrior's heart beats strong and swell.
Through the storm and through the strife,
Courage blossoms, bringing life.

With unyielding heart and fierce resolve,
In each battle, you evolve.
Stand tall against the fiercest gale,
For in your spirit, you shall prevail.

Through the blood and through the pain,
Honor the losses, cherish the gain.
Fight for truth, fight for light,
With the heart of a warrior, ignite.

When the world seems dark and cold,
Remember the stories of the bold.
You carry history in your veins,
Strength and pride in your refrains.

So rise up, with every breath,
Stand for love, defy the death.
In every heartbeat, hear the call,
You are a warrior, rise and fall.

Dance in the Storm

When the thunder cracks the sky,
Lift your head, let spirits fly.
In the rain, you find your grace,
Let the storm be your embrace.

Spin and twirl with wild delight,
In the chaos, feel the light.
Each drop a note, a song so sweet,
Dance with fervor, feel the beat.

Let the winds pull you along,
Every gust a brand new song.
With each step, cast out your fear,
In this storm, your heart's the spear.

As the clouds begin to clear,
Know that you have faced the fear.
Every tempest makes you strong,
In the rhythm, you belong.

So dance, oh soul, with fierce intent,
To the chorus of life, be content.
In the storm, you see your form,
A spirit wild, forever warm.

Transcending Limits

Beyond the walls that hold us tight,
We reach for stars, embrace the height.
Each voice a whisper, strong and clear,
Together we rise, dismissing fear.

In unity, we break the chains,
Our spirit flows like wild, free rains.
With every heartbeat, we redefine,
The bounds of life, where hope will shine.

Embrace the Challenge

When storms arise and shadows creep,
Stand tall and face the waves so deep.
Each trial holds a lesson true,
In every fall, there's strength in you.

The path ahead may twist and turn,
But in each step, a fire will burn.
With open heart and mind so wide,
Embrace the challenge, let it guide.

For every doubt that clouds your view,
Remember the courage born in you.
Rise up and let your spirit soar,
Success awaits beyond the door.

Through thick and thin, you'll find your way,
In darkest nights, you'll seek the day.
With every heartbeat, take the chance,
For life's a daring, bold romance.

So gather strength from deep within,
Face fear and let the journey begin.
The world is vast, your dreams are high,
Embrace the challenge, reach for the sky.

Unbreakable Will

In moments dark, when hope feels thin,
Remember the fire that burns within.
With every setback, grow more strong,
Your heart knows where it does belong.

Through storms of doubt that cloud your sight,
Hold tight to dreams that feel so right.
An unbreakable will, a guiding star,
You'll find your way, no matter how far.

The road is long, the journey tough,
But every step can be enough.
In whispered strength and quiet grace,
You'll conquer fears, you'll find your place.

With every fail, a lesson learned,
A brighter path begins to turn.
Embrace the fight, let courage flow,
Your spirit shines; let others know.

For you possess a heart of steel,
A force of nature, pure and real.
So rise again, with fire and thrill,
The world is yours — it craves your will.

Climb the Summit

Each mountain stands with peaks so bright,
A call to those who crave the height.
With every step, the air feels thin,
But strength grows deeper from within.

Embrace the climb, the steep ascent,
With every struggle, be content.
The summit waits, a chapter new,
A view so vast, reserved for you.

The path is rough, and stones may bite,
But hold your dreams in steady sight.
Each challenge faced, a step you take,
In every effort, a bond you make.

So breathe in deep, let courage rise,
With heart wide open, seek the skies.
The summit calls, your spirit's song,
With every heartbeat, you'll move along.

At last you stand, the top in view,
A testament to all you knew.
With arms outstretched, embrace the thrill,
You climbed the summit, proved your will.

The Light Within

In shadows cast by doubt and fear,
A spark ignites, a truth so clear.
The light within, so brave and bright,
Guides you through the darkest night.

Though storms may rage and winds may howl,
Listen close to your heart's sweet prowl.
A flame of hope that never wanes,
Through every struggle, joy remains.

The world can dim, but you can shine,
With every breath, your soul is fine.
The light within will show the way,
Embrace it fully; never sway.

Through trials faced and roads so long,
You'll find your strength, you'll find your song.
In every moment, let it glow,
For the light within is yours to show.

So, walk your path with heart aglow,
Let every heartbeat help you grow.
With faith and love, you'll be the spark,
The light within will chase the dark.

Discovering Depths

In waters deep and seldom seen,
Where shadows dance and dreams convene,
A whisper calls beneath the waves,
To venture forth, a heart it braves.

Explore the caves where secrets lie,
The echoes of the past drift by,
With open mind and steady hand,
We'll chart our course through untamed land.

Embrace the silence, let it speak,
In solitude, we find the unique,
Each ripple tells a tale so grand,
Of journeys taken, dreams so planned.

The depths we face, they shape our soul,
In darkness found, we become whole,
Through trials faced and fears laid bare,
We rise anew, a breath of air.

From ocean floors to sky's embrace,
We've sought the truth, we've found our place,
In depths discovered, light will shine,
Resilience found, a heart divine.

The Radiance of Resolve

In twilight's glow, where thoughts ignite,
A spark of hope breaks through the night,
With every challenge, courage grows,
A steadfast heart, it brightly glows.

Through storms of doubt, we'll stand our ground,
With voices raised, in strength we're found,
The path ahead may seem unclear,
But in our hearts, we hold the spear.

Each stumble brings a lesson learned,
With fiery passion, we have yearned,
To overcome the darkened skies,
And find the truth that never lies.

Embrace the fear, let it be fuel,
Our dreams, the compass; we'll not be the fool,
For in the struggle, light breaks through,
The radiance of resolve anew.

Together we'll step into the dawn,
Our spirits fierce, our hopes reborn,
With each new day, our flames will rise,
In the radiant glow, we claim the prize.

The Symphony of Growth

In silence falls the morning dew,
A freshness sings, the world anew,
Each breath a note, each step a key,
Together, we compose our plea.

From tender sprouts to towering trees,
In harmony, the whispers breeze,
Through seasons changing, we will thrive,
In every challenge, we'll survive.

The notes of patience, courage, grace,
Compose the canvas, time and space,
Each triumph small a part of sound,
In life's great orchestra, profound.

With every heartbeat, melodies play,
In symphonies of light and gray,
We grow and bend, yet stand so tall,
For in this dance, we rise, we fall.

Together we rise, in unison found,
A chorus of life, in joy resound,
Through trials faced and lessons penned,
The symphony of growth won't end.

Unfolding Your Vision

In every heart, a dream resides,
A glimmer bright, where hope abides,
Unfolding gently, like a flower,
Each petal speaks of inner power.

With vision clear, we take the stage,
A story unfolds, we turn the page,
Embrace the journey, trust the flow,
With every step, our spirits grow.

Lost in the haze of doubt and fear,
Remember why you ventured here,
In visions bright, we see the way,
To turn the night into the day.

Awakened dreams breathe life anew,
In colors vivid, bold, and true,
Let passion guide, let courage lead,
For in this path, we plant the seed.

Together we rise, hands intertwined,
With every heartbeat, worlds aligned,
In unfolding vision, we find our song,
A symphony of hope, we all belong.

Hearts Unleashed

With open hearts, we dance anew,
In rhythm soft, the world’s a view.
Each beat a promise, strong and bright,
Together we shine, igniting night.

Unfurl your wings, let courage sing,
In every moment, love's the spring.
We soar as one, through skies so wide,
In hearts unleashed, forever tied.

Defying the Odds

In the face of storms we stand,
Hearts ablaze, with dreams in hand.
Against the tide, we rise and fight,
With unwavering spirits, burning bright.

Every doubt that tries to bind,
We shake it off, leave it behind.
With courage deep, we take the leap,
A journey vast, not ours to keep.

Through tangled paths and rocky ways,
We push ahead, through darkest days.
With every scar, a story told,
Our futures shimmer, brave and bold.

In unity, we forge the path,
Facing fears, escaping wrath.
Together strong, we shatter chains,
Our laughter echoes, none remains.

Defying odds, we claim our fate,
With hope and strength, we celebrate.
For in the struggle, we will find,
A world anew, for hearts entwined.

The Whisper of Triumph

In moments whispered soft and low,
A tale of victory starts to grow.
With quiet steps, we move ahead,
The softest voice, the brave heart said.

An ember glows within the night,
Illuminating paths of light.
With every challenge, we find our way,
A spark ignites to seize the day.

Through trials faced, we learn to fly,
With wings of strength, we touch the sky.
Roots run deep, while branches sway,
In every heartbeat, dreams will play.

The road is long, but we will stand,
United whispers, hand in hand.
With every step, the promise grows,
In every heart, the triumph glows.

So here's to all who dare to dream,
Beneath the surface, hear the theme.
For in the stillness, we will thrive,
The whisper calls, alive, alive!

Forge Your Path

With shovels drawn, we stake our claim,
In lands unknown, we build our name.
Through every struggle, we take the stand,
Creating futures with steady hands.

The mountains high, the valleys low,
We carve our route, let courage grow.
With every choice, a lesson learned,
The fire of passion, fiercely burned.

In twilight's glow, we find our charge,
The road ahead begins to enlarge.
With dreams as maps, we wander wide,
Full of hope, and hearts filled with pride.

So lift your eyes to skies so vast,
Embrace the journey, hold it fast.
For in your hands, the power stays,
To forge your path in endless ways.

Though shadows loom and doubts may rise,
The star within you never lies.
Dare to dream, for life will show,
The vibrant trails where you will go.

Beyond the Shadows

In the whispers of dusk's sweet breath,
We find the light that conquers death.
Through every shadow, hope takes flight,
A beacon shining through the night.

With every heartbeat, patterns weave,
Stories told to those who believe.
Each trial faced, a chance to grow,
In depths of sorrow, strength will flow.

Through tangled paths, we journey on,
Into realms where fears are gone.
The dawning light, a promise bright,
Guides our souls through endless night.

Together strong, we break the mold,
In unity, our tales unfold.
From shadows deep, we rise as one,
To greet the warmth of a new sun.

Beyond the darkness, futures gleam,
A world awakened, alive with dream.
With voices raised, we sing our song,
In harmony, we all belong.

When Dreams Take Flight

In the twilight of the night,
Wings unfold, grasping for light.
Stars shimmer, guiding the way,
Heartbeats echo, urging to stay.

Visions dance on whispered breeze,
Hope ignites like rustling trees.
Chasing shadows, fears take flight,
Embracing worlds beyond our sight.

A canvas painted with bright hues,
Each stroke whispers tales to choose.
Infinite skies, horizons vast,
With every heartbeat, dreams hold fast.

Rivers of hope, flowing wide,
Carrying wishes side to side.
With eyes closed, we dare to soar,
Onward to the unknown shore.

Through valleys deep and mountains high,
We spread our wings, learning to fly.
For in the dreams, we find our might,
A journey kindled, burning bright.

Journey of Determination

Step by step, we brave the night,
With every stumble, we gain height.
Though the path may twist and bend,
Strength lies deep, our steadfast friend.

In shadows long, where doubts reside,
We push forward, with hearts open wide.
Each challenge faced, a lesson learned,
With every flame, our passion burned.

Through storms that rage and tides that turn,
The fire within continues to burn.
Holding dreams close, we won't depart,
Fueled by the rhythm of a brave heart.

The road stretches far, yet we press on,
With every dawn, a new hope is born.
In the company of courage, we’ll thrive,
The journey, a dance, keeps us alive.

With a compass true and a vision clear,
We march onwards, casting off fear.
The story unfolds, a tapestry spun,
In the journey of life, we’ve only begun.

A Canvas of Courage

Brush in hand, we paint our fate,
Each stroke a battle, fierce and great.
With colors bold, we shade our fears,
A masterpiece born from blood and tears.

The canvas waits for dreams to bloom,
In darkness deep, we forge our room.
With vibrant hues, we fight the night,
A tapestry woven in pure light.

Roots of Resilience

In the soil where dreams take root,
Strength emerges, resolute.
Through the storms that shake and sway,
From the ground, we find our way.

With branches reaching for the sky,
Leaves whisper truths as days go by.
Nurtured by tears, laughter, and pain,
Resilience blooms, again and again.

Through shadows thick and moments dark,
We savor the glow of each tiny spark.
In every challenge, we plant our seed,
Growing strong through every need.

The winds may howl, the earth may quake,
Yet deep within, we'll never break.
For in our hearts, the fire stays,
Lighting the path through life's harsh maze.

With roots so deep, intertwined with grace,
We stand firm, we face each trace.
In life's garden, we take our flight,
Embarking on journeys, pure and bright.

Chasing the Unattainable

Waves crash hard against the shore,
Dreams elude, yet we want more.
In the distance, shadows play,
Whispers call, pulling away.

Eyes set on the brilliant stars,
Mapping journeys, ranging far.
Each step forward, a fleeting chase,
For fleeting moments, we long to embrace.

In the mist, where hopes reside,
We explore paths, hearts open wide.
Every heartbeat a wishful song,
In the world of right and wrong.

Through valleys low and mountains high,
Each breath taken, we learn to fly.
Chasing dreams that seem so far,
In our hearts, we are the stars.

Though the unattainable is our quest,
In every struggle, we find our rest.
For in the chase, we truly find,
The beauty of dreams intertwined.

Steps Toward the Summit

One foot in front of the other,
Climbing each rugged stone,
The air grows thin, but I press on,
Determined to reach the throne.

The sun peeks over the ridge,
Casting shadows long and wide,
With each step, my heart races,
The summit waits, my guide.

Clouds gather like whispered dreams,
As I push through trials stark,
Each breath a vow to endure,
Each step ignites a spark.

The path winds like a ribbon,
Twisting through doubts and fear,
But deep within me awakens,
A strength that draws me near.

At last, I reach the summit,
Where the world is vast and free,
I stand in awe of creation,
And finally, I see me.

Voices of Resolve

In shadows where whispers linger,
A chorus rises bold and clear,
Voices of those who have faltered,
Yet shout against all the fear.

Each scar tells a story fiercer,
Of battles fought in silent night,
Weaving strength in every heartbeat,
Together, we step into light.

A melody builds in the distance,
With hope as its vibrant thread,
Through the clamor of despair,
A symphony of the led.

United, we march through the chaos,
Hand in hand, hearts ablaze,
With whispers turned to a thunder,
We carve out brighter days.

The echoes of past ignitions,
Resound in each fervent plea,
For voices of resolve awaken,
And together we are free.

Creating Tomorrow

With hands that mold the future,
We gather dreams to ignite,
Building bridges with kindness,
Crafting visions in the night.

The canvas of life unwritten,
Stretched wide before our gaze,
Each stroke a hope, each color,
A promise in the haze.

We plant seeds of compassion,
In the soil of love and care,
Tending to each tender sprout,
Knowing that we all share.

Each challenge is but a lesson,
A chance to rise and grow,
Creating tomorrow's beauty,
From the struggles we know.

Together, we forge a pathway,
Where laughter dances in the air,
In the garden of our making,
Where tomorrow blooms in flair.

Harnessing Possibilities

In the realm of endless chances,
We stand at the edge of dawn,
With dreams like bright balloons,
Yearning for flight, not drawn.

Ideas swirl like autumn leaves,
Restless in the morning breeze,
With open hearts, we gather strength,
Ready to grasp with ease.

Every doubt is a seedling,
Beneath the soil lies the fight,
We water it with courage,
To see our dreams take flight.

Construction of a vision grand,
Built from persistence and care,
We harness all our possibilities,
And rise above despair.

The canvas of our future waits,
For brushstrokes bold and bright,
With every heartbeat, we create,
Harnessing our shared light.

The Pulse of Progress

In every tick, a dream ignites,
Hearts align as hope takes flight.
With every step, the future sings,
A rhythm born from restless springs.

The gears of change begin to grind,
New paths emerge, our fates entwined.
Innovation sparks in the night,
A dawn of thought, a shared insight.

With courage drawn from lessons past,
We break the mold, our shadows cast.
Together we can break these walls,
A brighter world as darkness falls.

In unity, we find our voice,
Amidst the noise, we make our choice.
Through trials faced, we rise, we grow,
In the pulse of progress, we flow.

Navigating the Storm

When thunder roars and shadows creep,
We chart our course through waves so steep.
With sails unfurled, we greet the fray,
In tempest's howl, we find our way.

The winds may shift, the skies may cry,
But anchored hearts refuse to die.
Together bound, we stand as one,
A fierce resolve, our journey's spun.

Through turbulent tides, our spirits soar,
Each challenge faced, we learn to score.
The compass set, we trust our guide,
In the storm's eye, we dare abide.

With every lash of rain and gale,
We'll write a tale that will not pale.
In unity, our bond takes form,
Navigating through the storm.

Vision Unbound

In dreams we soar, beyond the stars,
A canvas vast, with no more scars.
Imagination lights the dark,
With every thought, we leave our mark.

We dare to chase what few have sought,
A tapestry of lessons taught.
With fearless hearts, our dreams expand,
A vision bright, we boldly stand.

Each whispering hope, a spark of fire,
With steady hands, we lift it higher.
In timeless realms, our stories blend,
With every curve, we transcend.

Through corridors of light we trod,
A truth revealed, a shared applaud.
With open minds, we break the round,
In the spaces vast, we are unbound.

The Spirit of Adventure

In wild terrains, where footsteps tread,
The call of fate, we journey ahead.
With hearts ablaze and spirits free,
The world unfolds, a tapestry.

From mountain peaks to ocean floor,
Every horizon whispers more.
With laughter shared and stories spun,
We chase the dawn, two souls as one.

Through thick and thin, we forge our path,
In moments bright, we find our laugh.
The road may twist, the skies may rain,
But every trial we shall gain.

In winding trails, we taste the thrill,
The spirit of adventure, a fervent will.
With every step, we live, we learn,
A rich and vibrant flame we burn.

The Blooming Path

Petals dance in morning light,
Whispers of a dream in flight.
Green leaves sway with softest grace,
Life awakens in this place.

Every step on this bright trail,
Guided by the sun's soft veil.
Colors touch the heart anew,
Nature’s canvas paints the view.

Gentle breezes hum a tune,
Underneath the watchful moon.
Every moment, pure delight,
In the glow of love and light.

Birds above take to the sky,
Freely soaring, oh so high.
Joyful laughter fills the air,
On this path, beyond compare.

With each bloom, new stories grow,
In their fragrance, hope will flow.
Together we will journey on,
To a place where dreams are drawn.

Finding Your North Star

In the night, a gleaming sign,
A guiding light, a thread divine.
Yearning hearts will seek the way,
To embrace a brand new day.

Whispers echo in the dark,
Follow truth; ignite that spark.
With each step, the path unfolds,
Stars above, their stories told.

Though the road may twist and turn,
Within your soul, the fire will burn.
Trust the journey, hold it tight,
Your North Star shines through the night.

Every doubt that clouds the mind,
Leave it behind; strength you'll find.
With courage, take a leap of faith,
Wonders wait on this path wreathed.

As the dawn begins to break,
Listen close; the world will wake.
In the light of day so clear,
Your North Star always will be near.

The Surge of Potential

In the silence, dreams await,
Hidden whispers form your fate.
Every heartbeat echoes strong,
A call to rise, to sing your song.

Mountains high, the valleys low,
Strength within begins to grow.
Harness power, chase the fire,
In your spirit, find desire.

Challenges will come your way,
Upon this path, do not sway.
Stand as one, unbreakable,
Feel the force; it's unmistakable.

With each step, break from the mold,
Set your fears and doubts controlled.
The surge within, fierce and bright,
Guide your journey through the night.

Embrace the light that fills your soul,
Reach for visions; make them whole.
In the end, you’ll come to see,
Your potential, wild and free.

Pathways to Freedom

In the shadows, chains dissolve,
With every heart, a spark to solve.
Voices rise, a chorus free,
Together forged in harmony.

Open doors to endless skies,
Where the spirit freely flies.
Winds of change on paths of grace,
Every step, a warm embrace.

Bridges built with love and care,
Bringing hope beyond despair.
Fear will crumble, truth revealed,
In this journey, wounds are healed.

With each choice, a trust reborn,
Out of darkness, hope is sworn.
Casting doubts into the sea,
A life embraced, unbound and free.

Now the road stretches ahead,
With dreams ignited, hearts are fed.
Walking boldly hand in hand,
Together, we will take a stand.

Voice of the Brave

In shadows deep, they stand with pride,
Voices rise, no fear to hide.
With every word, they shift the night,
The brave ignite the world with light.

Through trials faced, they bear the cost,
For every gain, something is lost.
Yet still they stand, together, strong,
Their hearts unite, a timeless song.

In whispers soft, or shouts so loud,
Their voices echo, fierce and proud.
From ashes born, they find their way,
A testament to every day.

Through storms they march, through pain and strife,
With hope in hand, they shape their life.
Bound by trust, they blaze the trail,
In every heart, the brave prevail.

So hear the call, let courage soar,
Embrace the fight, and seek for more.
For in the end, together they thrive,
With voices strong, the brave survive.

The Summit Beckons

High above, the peak awaits,
A call to climb, to test the fates.
With every step, the view expands,
Each moment forged by nature's hands.

The pathwinds up through mist and stone,
Where fears are faced, and seeds are sown.
The summit beckons, bold and bright,
A dream to chase, a guiding light.

Through jagged rocks and chilling air,
The brave embrace the weight they bear.
With sweat and grit, they fight the urge,
To rise above, to stand, emerge.

At journey's end, the glory's theirs,
They stand as one, unbound by cares.
Views stretch beyond, horizons wide,
In unity, they take the pride.

For every summit reached, they know,
The climb itself fuels strength to grow.
With hearts ablaze, they seize the day,
The summit waits, just step away.

Against the Tide

Waves crash hard on rugged shore,
Yet still they fight, seek to restore.
With every push, the tide recedes,
They find their ground, plant steadfast seeds.

In currents fierce, they find their way,
Resilience guides, they choose to stay.
No fear of depths, nor stormy skies,
With open hearts, they recognize.

Every setback fuels their drive,
In struggle deep, they learn to thrive.
Together strong, they stand as one,
With every battle, they find the sun.

Through darkest nights, they hold their ground,
In unity, their strength is found.
They face the tide, they face the storm,
With courage bold, their spirits warm.

So when the waves rise high and wild,
Know that the brave, they'll not be mild.
Against the tide, they stand, they roar,
With every step, they seek for more.

A Symphony of Strength

In quiet moments, strength unfolds,
A symphony where stories told.
Each note a chord of hope and grace,
In every heartbeat, find your place.

With hands entwined, they lift the sound,
In harmony, their hearts are bound.
Resilience plays a vital role,
In the symphony, they find their soul.

Through highs and lows, the music swells,
In shared embrace, the magic dwells.
Together fierce, like thunder's call,
A crescendo that can never fall.

In every trial, a sweeter tone,
In every challenge, they have grown.
The rhythm of hope, the pulse of fight,
In this grand symphony, ignite the light.

So let the notes of strength resound,
In hearts and minds, let peace be found.
For in this music, lives entwined,
A symphony of strength defined.

The Fire That Burns

In the heart lies a glowing flame,
Flickering whispers of hope and pain.
It dances wild, it knows no chains,
In every soul, it leaves a stain.

Through the night, it lights the way,
A beacon bright when skies are gray.
Fear it not, for it ignites,
The passion deep, the fiery rights.

It spreads its warmth to those in need,
A source of strength, a noble creed.
With every spark, a story told,
Of dreams and wishes, brave and bold.

Yet in its wake, shadows may fall,
A double-edged sword, it conquers all.
To harness well, we must discern,
The love, the pain, the fire that burns.

So nurture it with gentle care,
For in shared hearts, we find our flare.
Together strong, we'll face the night,
And from the fire, we'll share the light.

Limitless Horizons

The sun breaks free, a brand-new day,
Painting the sky in hues of play.
Mountains call with whispers clear,
Endless paths, no room for fear.

Waves crash soft on distant shores,
Each grain of sand, a world that soars.
With open hearts, we chase the dawn,
In every step, we feel reborn.

The winds may change, but we hold fast,
In every moment, our fears are past.
With dreams in hand, we sail afar,
To find our place beneath the stars.

Through valleys deep and forests wide,
The soul awakens with the tide.
To seek the skies where eagles fly,
Embracing all, our spirits high.

Limitless horizons, bright and bold,
Every journey, a story told.
With every breath, we break the mold,
In unity, our dreams unfold.

Unstoppable Journey

Step by step, we forge our fate,
With hearts aglow, we navigate.
Through twisting paths and rivers wide,
In every heartbeat, love's our guide.

Over mountains, through the storm,
In unity, our spirits warm.
Each challenge met, a battle won,
Together, we embrace the sun.

Time may test our every wish,
But in the depth, our hopes persist.
With every trial, we grow more strong,
In harmony, we sing our song.

Each memory, a stepping stone,
In every dark, we find our own.
With courage fierce, we rise above,
An unstoppable journey, fueled by love.

So let us dance through life's embrace,
With open hearts, we find our place.
In every moment, we are free,
Together bound, just you and me.

Echoes of Courage

In silent whispers, courage speaks,
In hearts of those who dare to seek.
With every step, old fears dissolve,
In the pursuit, our souls evolve.

The shadows linger, yet we stand,
With open hearts and steady hands.
Through trials fierce, we pave the way,
In echoes loud, we find our say.

Beneath the weight of doubts that cling,
Resilience blooms, a vibrant spring.
In every scar, a story shines,
Of battles fought and lofty climbs.

With voices strong, we rise as one,
To face the storms, to face the sun.
In every whisper, truth resounds,
In echoes of courage, hope abounds.

So let us sing our battle song,
In unity, we all belong.
With brave hearts open, we will endure,
In echoes of courage, we are sure.

Steps of Faith

In shadows deep, our hearts ignite,
We tread the path, guided by light.
Every step, a whispered prayer,
In trust we find, His presence there.

With heavy hearts, we face the night,
Yet courage blooms, we stand upright.
Each stumble leads to lessons learned,
A flame of hope within us burns.

Together as we walk this way,
We share our fears, we share our day.
In faith we rise, our spirits soar,
Through storms we'll seek an open door.

Hand in hand, through valleys wide,
We meet the dawn, cast doubts aside.
A journey forged with love and grace,
In every challenge, find our place.

So step by step, we'll move ahead,
With every prayer, by courage led.
The road is long, but hearts won't wane,
In faith united, we will reign.

A Tapestry of Triumph

Threads of courage, woven tight,
We stitch our dreams into the night.
Each color bright, a tale begun,
Together, we rise, we shine like sun.

In every challenge, beauty found,
A tapestry, with love is bound.
As life unfolds, our stories blend,
With every stitch, our spirits mend.

Moments shared of joy and pain,
Together in sunshine, together in rain.
With bold designs, we paint the skies,
A vibrant life, where hope defies.

As we embrace the unknown road,
Our hearts ablaze, we share the load.
With every thread, we weave our fate,
In unity, we celebrate.

Through trials faced, resilience glows,
In tapestry, our strength just grows.
Each triumph shines, a work of art,
In woven dreams, we play our part.

The Road Ahead

A winding path, the journey calls,
With every step, the spirit sprawls.
The road ahead, unknown yet near,
In every turn, a spark of cheer.

Beneath the stars, our hopes align,
With faith as guide, our hearts entwine.
Through shadows cast and sunlight bright,
We pave our way, with dreams in sight.

The rhythm of the world, we feel,
In every challenge, strength revealed.
Together strong, we face the day,
With love as compass, come what may.

As mountains rise and valleys dip,
We hold on tight, we fear not slip.
In unity, our voices blend,
With each new dawn, our spirits mend.

The road ahead, a canvas bare,
We'll paint our dreams, lay every care.
With open hearts, we journey on,
In every step, a brave new dawn.

Uncharted Territory

Beyond the maps, we roam so free,
In uncharted lands, just you and me.
With open minds and hearts aglow,
Together, we'll explore the flow.

Every whisper of the trees,
Every song upon the breeze.
Each moment sparks a brand new quest,
In nature's arms, we find our rest.

Curious stars in the vast night sky,
As we wander, we learn to fly.
In landscapes strange, our spirits grow,
With every step, new wonders show.

Through rivers wide and mountains steep,
We tread the path, our dreams to keep.
In every heartbeat, adventure calls,
In uncharted lands, the joy befalls.

So hand in hand, dear friend of mine,
In every moment, we will shine.
The world awaits, our journeys share,
In uncharted territory, we declare.

Rise to the Challenge

Awake with the dawn's gentle light,
Face the battles you must fight.
With courage that ignites the flame,
Each new struggle builds your name.

Step forward into the unknown,
With grit and heart, you will have grown.
The path may twist, the ground may shake,
But only then, true strength you'll make.

When doubt begins to take its toll,
Remember the fire in your soul.
With every fall, you rise anew,
A warrior strong, forever true.

Let whispers of fear fade away,
Trust in yourself, seize the day.
The summit waits, your dreams in sight,
So rise to the challenge, shine so bright.

Every step, a victory gained,
Though trails are tough and uncontained.
With heart ablaze and spirit bold,
Your story of courage will be told.

Unseen Strengths

Beneath the surface, power lies,
Hidden depths where courage flies.
In silence blooms a quiet force,
Charting paths, a steady course.

When shadows loom and fears arise,
Look within to claim your prize.
For every doubt, a spark will blaze,
Your heart ignites in nuanced ways.

In moments where you feel alone,
Remember strengths you’ve always known.
Unseen wings will help you soar,
With every challenge, find much more.

The journey's made of twists and turns,
In every fall, a lesson learns.
Embrace the power still untapped,
A treasure worth, no heart enwrapped.

So seek the light in shadows cast,
Let unseen strengths free at last.
With every heartbeat, rise anew,
Unveil the strength that lives in you.

Embrace the Climb

The mountain stands, so tall, so grand,
A challenge waits, a call to stand.
With every step, the view expands,
Embrace the climb, it's in your hands.

Armored by hope, you scale each height,
With spirit fierce, heart filled with light.
The journey winds, but you won't tremble,
Strength in your soul, an endless ember.

The air grows thin, yet you persist,
With focus sharp, you can't resist.
Each hurdle crossed, a badge of pride,
In unity with the path you guide.

If clouds should gather, storms arise,
Remember the strength that's in your eyes.
For challenges mold who we can be,
Embrace the climb, and you will see.

Atop the peak, a world unfolds,
The tales of courage, ripe and bold.
In every moment, rise and strive,
Embrace the climb, feel bliss alive.

Boundless Horizons

Beyond the limits, dreams take flight,
In endless skies, the stars are bright.
With every heartbeat, horizons wide,
Feel the universe as your guide.

With open hearts, we seek the new,
Adventure calls, it's calling you.
Beyond the shores, where hopes reside,
A canvas stretched, where dreams abide.

The journey teaches, wisdom grows,
Through valleys low and peaks that glow.
Boundless horizons, ever near,
With every step, release your fear.

As waves of change wash over land,
Together, we rise, united we stand.
For every dawn that breaks anew,
Claim what’s waiting, let it ensue.

So chase the sun and dance with fate,
In boundless horizons, dream's estate.
With arms wide open, take the chance,
Embrace the journey, join the dance.

Wings of Ambition

With dreams like eagles soaring high,
We chase the stars, we touch the sky.
Each challenge met, we rise again,
Fueled by the fire that burns within.

In the winds of change, we learn to glide,
With every step, we break the tide.
No chains can hold, no doubts can bind,
The heart of those who seek and find.

From shadows cast in doubt's domain,
We'll find the strength to face the strain.
Our vision clear, our spirits bold,
A tale of triumph yet untold.

The journey long, the path unsure,
But with each risk, our dreams secure.
With wings of ambition, hearts ablaze,
We'll forge our fate in radiant rays.

So let us rise, above the fray,
On wings of hope, we'll find our way.
In every heartbeat, every breath,
Our ambitions soar, defying death.

The Call to Believe

In whispers soft, the dreamers speak,
With every hope, a future we seek.
Through darkest nights, through endless days,
We find our strength in faith's embrace.

For when the doubt begins to creep,
And shadows stir where comfort sleeps,
The call to believe ignites the heart,
A guiding light, a work of art.

Through valleys low and mountains high,
We'll raise our voices to the sky.
With every challenge we will stand,
United strong, hand in hand.

The seeds of doubt will not take root,
In fertile soil where dreams are put.
With courage sewn, our dreams will grow,
The beauty found in every flow.

So let us rise, our hopes entwined,
With faith as fuel, our paths aligned.
In every heart, a light will shine,
The call to believe, forever divine.

In the Face of Fear

When shadows loom and whispers freeze,
We stand our ground, we bend the knees.
In the face of fear, we find our might,
A flicker deep, a guiding light.

With every trial, we learn to fight,
Through darkest storms, we seek the light.
Each heartbeat echoes, loud and clear,
Resilience forged in grip of fear.

The mountains high, the valleys deep,
In courage found, we'll take the leap.
For every fear that's faced today,
Is strength renewed along the way.

So rise we must, through doubt and dread,
With fearless hearts, a life well-led.
We'll face the storms, we'll walk the night,
In the face of fear, we'll find our light.

For courage blooms where terror lies,
In every heart, a spirit cries.
So hand in hand, we’ll face the dawn,
In the face of fear, we carry on.

Grounded in Hope

Upon the earth, our roots run deep,
In soil enriched, our dreams will leap.
With eyes on skies, yet hearts below,
We hold the dreams and let them grow.

In moments still, in whispered air,
We plant our seeds, show love and care.
With every trial, our spirits rise,
Grounded in hope, we'll touch the skies.

For every storm that shakes the ground,
A deeper strength in us is found.
With every laugh, with every tear,
Our roots entwine, we persevere.

So when the winds begin to roar,
And doubts arise like waves ashore,
We'll stand our ground, hands held up high,
Grounded in hope, we'll never shy.

For love's embrace will lead us through,
In every heart, a life anew.
United strong, no fear can sway,
Grounded in hope, we find our way.

Echoes of Potential

In shadows where dreams quietly dwell,
Whispers of hope begin to swell.
A spark ignites the hidden flame,
And echoes arise, calling your name.

With each step forward, the world aligns,
Endless paths weave through time's designs.
Silent strength in hearts untold,
A tapestry of courage unfolds.

Through storms that threaten, skies that rage,
The heart learns to turn the page.
In every doubt, in every fear,
Resilience blooms, bright and clear.

Awakened visions stretch out wide,
Seizing the moment, not just the tide.
With every heartbeat, each truth unfolds,
A symphony of stories, waiting to be told.

So listen closely, to the call within,
The journey starts where new dreams begin.
Embrace the echoes, let them guide,
For within your soul, the future resides.

Carve Your Future

With hands of stone and dreams of clay,
Mold the life you wish to stay.
Each choice you make, a chisel sharp,
Sculpting visions, lighting the dark.

In the quiet hours, find your voice,
Rise from the ashes, make your choice.
The canvas waits, wide and clear,
Paint your story, without fear.

Shatter the limits that bind your mind,
Seek the wonders that you will find.
Through valleys low, and mountains high,
Your spirit soars, it's time to fly.

Nurture passions, let them bloom,
Create a path, dispel the gloom.
With every effort, every plan,
You shape the world, be the artist's hand.

So step by step, with faith so true,
Carve the future that lives in you.
Embrace the journey, leave your mark,
In every moment, ignite the spark.

The Heart's Odyssey

In the depths of an endless sea,
A heart sets sail, wild and free.
With every wave, a tale is spun,
Through tempests fierce, the journey's begun.

Guided by stars through the night,
In quiet whispers, dreams take flight.
A compass forged from love and pain,
Navigating joy, navigating rain.

Islands of hope dot the vast expanse,
Each encounter, a serendipitous chance.
With open eyes and open heart,
The odyssey blooms, a work of art.

Beneath the surface where secrets lie,
Emerald depths, where fears can die.
Embrace the unknown, let it unfold,
The heart’s true treasure turned to gold.

So sail on, through the tides of time,
In every rhythm, in every rhyme.
For the journey within is where you'll see,
The heart's true odyssey, wild and free.

Shifting the Paradigm

Through lenses of change, the world appears,
Old ways dissolve, confronting fears.
With every shift, new truths arise,
Breaking the rules, opening eyes.

In patterns woven, threads untwine,
A tapestry of thought, so divine.
Voices merge, a harmony grows,
Together we stand, this truth bestows.

In the dance of progress, we find our song,
Challenging norms, where we belong.
With hearts aligned and spirits strong,
Shifting the paradigm, righting the wrongs.

Embrace the chaos, the world is wide,
In every challenge, let hope reside.
For in transformation, breakthroughs bloom,
Lighting the way, dispelling the gloom.

So take a step towards what you seek,
In every whisper, in every peak.
Together we build, redefine, aspire,
Shifting the paradigm, igniting the fire.

Embracing the Unknown

In shadows deep, we take our flight,
A path unworn, but full of light.
With hearts aglow, we face the breeze,
Embracing fate, our souls at ease.

The whispers call, the stars align,
In every step, new worlds combine.
Each twist and turn, a treasure sought,
In silence found, all hope is caught.

From doubt we rise, our spirit strong,
In every note, we find our song.
With courage bold, we forge ahead,
On paths unknown, our dreams are spread.

Through mist and fog, we wander wide,
With open hearts, we shall abide.
The journey holds a sacred key,
Unlocking all that we can be.

A Tapestry of Hope

In every thread, a story weaves,
A dance of light that never leaves.
Colors bright, in harmony,
Together they speak symphony.

Each hue reflects a tale of grace,
Where dreams and fears take tender space.
With hands that stitch through joy and strife,
We craft the patterns of our life.

With every tear, a strength revealed,
In fragile seams, our hearts are healed.
A fabric rich with laughter's sound,
In woven love, our peace is found.

Through storms that rage and winds that wail,
This tapestry shall not grow pale.
Together bound, our spirits soar,
A timeless hope, forevermore.

Flames of Aspiration

In embers glow, we find our spark,
With fervent hearts, we light the dark.
The fire within begins to swell,
A beacon bright, our dreams to tell.

With every flicker, passions rise,
Igniting visions in the skies.
With purpose bold, we chase the blaze,
With every breath, we set ablaze.

In courage drawn from deep inside,
We face the winds, we will not hide.
For every flame, a story's flame,
In unity, we play the game.

Through trials faced, the heat may grow,
But in those flames, our spirits glow.
Together we ignite the day,
In flames of hope, we find our way.

The Strength Within

In quiet moments, strength is found,
In whispered thoughts, our hearts unbound.
Like roots that reach beneath the soil,
We flourish strong, we rise from toil.

With every challenge, we will stand,
A fortress built on steady land.
Our spirits soar like eagles high,
With wings spread wide, we touch the sky.

For in the depths, our power lies,
Through storms we feel, through darkest skies.
With hope ignited, we shall rise,
A testament beneath the skies.

Together forged, our hearts entwined,
In unity, our strength defined.
With voices strong, we face the night,
The strength within will be our light.

Building Bridges to Tomorrow

With every stone we place, we rise,
Crafting paths toward the blue skies.
Hope and dreams in our hands hold,
Together we brave, together we're bold.

Across the rivers of doubt we stride,
In unity found, we take it in pride.
The future sparkles just out of sight,
With each step forward, we ignite the light.

Hands joined tightly, hearts open wide,
In this journey, we will not hide.
Through struggles faced, we find our way,
Building bridges to a brighter day.

As the sun sets on the troubled past,
We look ahead, our bond will last.
With every kindness, every cheer,
We shape the world, erase the fear.

Together we rise, as one we soar,
Through the challenges, we will explore.
This bridge we build will never break,
For tomorrow's promise is ours to make.

A Journey of Many Steps

Each step we take brings us near,
Faces of joy, whispers of cheer.
With every turn, a story unfolds,
In the warmth of hearts, adventure molds.

The path is winding, at times unclear,
Yet forward we move, void of fear.
Through valleys deep and mountains high,
A tapestry woven, beneath the sky.

With friends beside, the load feels light,
Together we seek, together we fight.
The road may twist, yet we persist,
For moments shared are too sweet to miss.

Our feet may tire, but spirits stay strong,
In this great dance, we all belong.
With laughter ringing, dreams take flight,
This journey of ours shines ever bright.

So take my hand, let's wander free,
The world is vast, a wondrous sea.
With every step in sync, we chase,
A journey defined by love and grace.

The Realm Beyond Fear

In shadows deep, fear starts to creep,
But hope shines on, no need to weep.
With courage found, we break the chains,
In the light of dawn, resilience reigns.

Journey forth to the realm unknown,
Where dreams are sown, and seeds are grown.
Beyond the veil where fears reside,
A treasure waits on the other side.

With every heartbeat, we make the leap,
To conquer doubts, our spirits keep.
In the dance of risk and sweet delight,
The realm beyond fear glows ever bright.

Together we stand, hand in hand,
In this bold place, we make our stand.
With hearts as shields, we face the night,
Finding our way in the starlit flight.

So rise, dear soul, let courage steer,
The journey unfolds when we persevere.
In the realm beyond, we shall find bliss,
In places where fear ceases to exist.

Whispers of Potential

In the quiet hours, potential sings,
Soft, subtle truths, like gentle wings.
With every breath, a spark ignites,
Whispers of dreams that reach new heights.

Within our hearts, a treasure lies,
Hidden gems beneath the skies.
With courage fueled by love's embrace,
We dance in time, we find our place.

The world awaits, with arms spread wide,
In every challenge, we take in stride.
With minds aligned, and spirits true,
The whispers call, they beckon you.

Through trials faced and mountains climbed,
Each step we take, we've grown and rhymed.
In unity, we hear the call,
Potential blooms, and we stand tall.

So heed the whispers, let them guide,
In this vast world, together we'll glide.
With open hearts and dreams that soar,
We are the potential, forevermore.

Ignite Your Fire

In the quiet of the night,
A spark begins to glow.
Deep inside, a flame ignites,
And urges you to grow.

Feel the warmth that starts to rise,
Beneath the thickened skin.
Let your courage touch the sky,
Embrace the fire within.

Every doubt like ashes falls,
While hope begins to soar.
With each heartbeat, hear the calls,
To light a path once more.

As you breathe, the flames expand,
And dance within your soul.
Hold your dreams with steady hands,
And let the passion roll.

So ignite your fire bright,
And let the world behold.
The strength you find in darkest night,
Is worth its weight in gold.

The Path Within

In shadows deep, where secrets lie,
A whisper calls your name.
Through twisted paths, where shadows sigh,
You seek to spark the flame.

With every step, embrace your truth,
A journey carved by heart.
The echoes of your ancient youth,
Will guide each vital part.

The turns may twist, the road may bend,
But trust where it may go.
Within the heart, all dreams transcend,
And wisdom starts to flow.

Let go of fears that bind you tight,
And tread with gentle grace.
For in your soul, a guiding light,
Illuminates your place.

So walk the path that lies within,
With courage in your stride.
For every loss, there comes a win,
When faith becomes your guide.

Wings of Perseverance

When storms arise, and shadows fall,
Stand tall and face the fight.
With every bruise, you hear the call,
To rise and claim your right.

The weight of doubt may press you down,
Yet hope will keep you strong.
With open heart, you'll wear the crown,
And prove where you belong.

In the chaos, find your peace,
As struggles shape your way.
With every tear, you find release,
To greet a brighter day.

So spread your wings, and soar above,
The trials that you face.
For in the end, it's strength and love
That grant you true embrace.

Embrace the winds that push and pull,
Let perseverance guide.
With wings of hope, your heart is full,
Your spirit will abide.

Steps of Resolve

Each step you take, a vow you make,
To seek what feels so right.
Through every challenge, every ache,
You'll shine with inner light.

When doubts arise and courage fades,
Remember why you came.
For every journey that cascades,
Is born from passion's flame.

The road is long, but not in vain,
With heartbeats as your guide.
Through laughter's charm and sorrow's rain,
Your spirit will abide.

So tread with strength, and hold your ground,
For purpose fuels your stride.
In every step, the truth is found,
As dreams become your pride.

With every stride, declare your path,
And let your vision steer.
With steps of hope, you conquer wrath,
Your spirit knows no fear.

Scaling New Heights

With every step, we brave the grind,
Reaching peaks we've yet to find.
The air is thin, but spirits soar,
Together we'll unlock each door.

The view from here takes breath away,
Sunlight dances, end of day.
Emboldened hearts, we leap and strive,
Our passion fuels, we feel alive.

Through whispers of the mountain's lore,
We challenge limits, seek for more.
Each trial faced, we stand as one,
A journey shared, our race begun.

Beyond the clouds, the sky does call,
We rise above, we stand so tall.
With hope and grit, we forge our way,
Scaling new heights, seize the day.

In laughter shared, our fears dissolve,
In every climb, our dreams evolve.
We'll chase the stars, find paths anew,
Scaling heights, with skies so blue.

Dreams in Motion

In corners dark, our hopes take flight,
With whispered dreams that chase the night.
They flicker bright, the stars align,
In motion now, our spirits shine.

Like rivers flowing, always wide,
Our visions dance, they swell with pride.
Together we'll ignite the flame,
Our hearts ablaze, we'll stake our claim.

Beneath the moon, our plans unfold,
In moments bright, the future bold.
Through valleys deep and mountains high,
We'll find a way to reach the sky.

The world spins fast, our dreams don't rest,
In every heart, we chase the quest.
A journey shared, no path too long,
In dreams in motion, we belong.

With hands held tight, we break the mold,
Our story bright, a tale retold.
We'll paint the sky and make it true,
In dreams in motion, me and you.

The Art of Tenacity

In shadows cast, we learn to fight,
With every fall, we reach for light.
Resilient hearts, we stand so strong,
In the art of tenacity, we belong.

Through stormy seas and rugged shores,
Our spirit sings, and hope restores.
Each setback faced, we rise anew,
With grit and grace, we’ll push right through.

In every challenge, lessons gleam,
We’ll forge our path, we’ll live our dream.
With steadfast will, our souls ignite,
The art of tenacity shines bright.

Together we’ll defy the odds,
With steadfast hearts and hopeful nods.
We'll paint our futures, bold and free,
In tenacity, we find the key.

In every struggle, strength we find,
Through tears and joy, our fates entwined.
With every step, we build our way,
The art of tenacity, our play.

Embers of Ambition

In quiet nights, a spark ignites,
The embers glow, the future writes.
With courage, dreams begin to swell,
In whispers soft, we weave our spell.

Each vision cast, a guiding star,
With every step, we'll journey far.
Through winding paths, our fire grows,
In embers warm, our passion flows.

The world awaits, its canvas bare,
With palettes bold, we'll paint with care.
Our hearts ablaze, ambition clear,
With every breath, we conquer fear.

Through trials faced, our flames will dance,
In unity, we take our chance.
With hands entwined, we'll light the night,
In embers of ambition, we take flight.

With every dream, a tale unfolds,
In fervent hearts, our purpose holds.
Together now, we rise and shine,
Embers of ambition, we define.

Strength in Vulnerability

In shadows deep, we find our grace,
A tender heart, a warm embrace.
To be undone, yet still stand tall,
In honest truth, we break the fall.

The cracks we bear, the wounds we show,
Are paths to light, where love can grow.
With every tear, a strength is born,
In fragile moments, hope is worn.

The courage found in quiet tears,
Unveils the depth of all our fears.
Embracing pain, we touch the sky,
In vulnerability, we learn to fly.

So here we stand, in gentle bounds,
With every heartbeat, wisdom sounds.
A tapestry of scars we weave,
In strength of soul, we dare believe.

Through aching nights and tender dawns,
The beauty shines, our spirit drawn.
In strength, we find a world anew,
In vulnerability, we break through.

Triumph Awaits

Upon the hill, the sun will rise,
With every dream, we touch the skies.
The road ahead may twist and turn,
But in our hearts, the fire will burn.

With every step, the world we chase,
In trials faced, we find our place.
The whispers say, 'You are enough,'
In strength of will, we rise from tough.

The mountains loom, but we won't yield,
With hope as armor, fate our shield.
Each challenge met, a lesson gained,
In every scar, our strength is claimed.

With voices strong, we lift the flame,
Embracing all, we stake our claim.
In unity, our spirits soar,
With hearts ablaze, we seek for more.

So take my hand, together we stand,
With dreams ignited, futures planned.
The path is bright, our spirits light,
In every pulse, triumph ignites.

Breaking Barriers

With every word, we tear the wall,
United hearts will never fall.
The strength of many, one pure voice,
In every struggle, we rejoice.

The chains that bind, we cast away,
In unity, we pave the way.
For every silence, we speak loud,
In breaking barriers, we are proud.

Doubt may linger, shadows might creep,
But in our dreams, we find our leap.
With every pulse, the world can feel,
Our spirits soar, our hopes are real.

Together we rise, hand in hand,
With every heartbeat, we take a stand.
In love’s embrace, we find our might,
With courage born, we claim our right.

So let the world know our name,
In every heart, ignite the flame.
For breaking barriers, we unite,
In every challenge, we see the light.

Rise from Ashes

From dust we come, to dust we rise,
In twilight's arms, the phoenix flies.
With every ember, rebirth calls,
In shattered dreams, our spirit thralls.

In darkest nights, hope finds a spark,
With each new dawn, we light the dark.
The ashes speak of battles fought,
In every loss, a lesson taught.

With scars adorned, we wear our pride,
The journey long, yet dreams abide.
With every breath, we claim our fate,
In whispers soft, we cultivate.

So rise, dear soul, from what was lost,
In every trial, we pay the cost.
With hearts ablaze, the world awaits,
For from the ashes, triumph states.

Embrace the change, let go the past,
With open arms, our joys amassed.
In every moment, life's sweet song,
We rise from ashes, bold and strong.

Beyond the Boundaries

In shadows cast by doubt, we stand,
With dreams that stretch beyond this land.
The stars above, a guiding light,
Awaits the brave who chase the night.

Each step we take, a new frontier,
With courage rooted, free from fear.
Together we will break the chains,
And rise above the endless plains.

The journey calls, with whispers sweet,
In every heartbeat, it's our feat.
We'll step beyond familiar skies,
And let our hopes learn how to fly.

Through valleys deep and mountains high,
We find our strength; we dare to try.
With every risk, a world unfolds,
A tapestry of dreams retold.

So let us roam, let's take the chance,
With open hearts, in wild romance.
Beyond the boundaries, futures gleam,
In every challenge lies a dream.

Echoes of Potential

Within each heart, a rhythm beats,
A silent call, where courage greets.
The echoes linger, yet unheard,
A song of dreams, a whispered word.

The paths we walk, both rough and wide,
Contain the spark we often hide.
With every step, we trade our fears,
For brighter days, through whispered years.

Our potential glows, a fiery seam,
Binding together each shared dream.
When lifted high, the voices blend,
A symphony that will not end.

So heed the call that's deep inside,
The echoes urge you, do not hide.
For in the depths, we seek the lore,
Of who we are and so much more.

In every heart, the light doth play,
Be bold, embrace it; seize the day.
For life's a canvas vast and bright,
And you, dear soul, are purest light.

Ignite Your Passion

A flicker grows within your core,
A flame awakened, wanting more.
In every heartbeat, feel the heat,
Your passions bloom, your spirit greet.

With unwavering zest, rise and shine,
Embrace the dreams that intertwine.
In colors bold, let's paint the skies,
And watch our visions come alive.

Through trials faced, we hone our art,
A dance of hope, a brand new start.
For every spark ignites a blaze,
In passion's grip, you'll find your ways.

Let nothing dim the fire inside,
With open hearts, let's take the ride.
With every step, we forge our fate,
To let the world know we create.

Ignite your passion, make it soar,
Unlock the doors and hear the roar.
For as we dream, the world awakes,
And magic blooms in every shape.

Trust the Journey

Through winding roads and skies unknown,
With every step, our courage grown.
Each moment, filled with lessons true,
In every path, we find anew.

So trust the journey; feel its grace,
As time unfolds, we find our place.
In laughter shared and tears we sow,
The seeds of faith begin to grow.

A tapestry of trials faced,
Will guide us on with gentle haste.
For obstacles, like waves, will pass,
And in their wake, we'll find our glass.

In joy and pain, we take the ride,
For life’s a journey, not a guide.
With open hearts, we’ll brave the storm,
And trust the journey keeps us warm.

So take my hand, walk by my side,
Together let’s embrace the tide.
With every heartbeat, memories weave,
In trust, the journey we believe.

Seeds of Resilience

In the earth, a promise lies,
Beneath the stormy, grayened skies.
Roots dig deep, through pain and strife,
Nurtured dreams embrace new life.

Each seed a story, love and care,
Whispers of hope linger in the air.
Through trials faced, we rise anew,
In the heart, resilience grew.

Branches stretch towards the sun,
Together strong, we've just begun.
United blooms, in colors bright,
In unity, we find our light.

Even in shadows, strength we find,
With every challenge, hearts aligned.
The winds may blow, the rains may fall,
But from the depths, we will stand tall.

So plant your dreams, let courage flow,
Through darkened days, let faith still glow.
For every end, a new embrace,
From seeds of hope, we find our place.

Chart Your Course

The stars above begin to shine,
A map of dreams, both yours and mine.
With compass set and sails unfurled,
We venture forth to seek the world.

Through waves that crash and winds that blow,
Each path we take helps us to grow.
The horizon calls, a siren's song,
In every heartbeat, we belong.

Navigate with heart and mind,
For in each challenge, strength we find.
The journey's long, the road unsealed,
But with each step, our fate revealed.

Trust the whispers of your soul,
In every moment, you are whole.
Let intuition light your way,
And guide you through both night and day.

So chart your course, embrace the thrill,
For every dream, there lies a skill.
With passion fierce and minds aligned,
We'll find our way, let fate be kind.

The Pulse of Possibility

In every heartbeat, a tale unfolds,
A dance of dreams yet to be told.
Potential sparkles in the air,
A canvas blank, stripped of despair.

The world invites us to explore,
With open hearts, we can restore.
Each choice we make, a step towards light,
In shadows deep, we find our might.

In whispers soft, the future calls,
Through peaks of joy and twilight falls.
The pulse of hope, it flows within,
Each breath a chance to begin again.

So seize the moment, paint your sky,
With colors bright, let spirits fly.
The rhythm of life sings loud and clear,
In every loss, there lies a cheer.

Embrace the unknown, let fears dissolve,
In every heart, new worlds involve.
For in each pulse, possibility thrives,
In the embrace of dreams, we're alive.

Fearless Ascent

Step by step, ascend the height,
With courage fierce, embrace the fight.
Each peak looms large, yet small we stand,
In unity, we reach for land.

The path may twist, the world may shake,
But faith ignites the steps we take.
In every stumble, strength is born,
With hearts ablaze, each day is worn.

The summit calls, a vision clear,
With every breath, we draw it near.
Fearless spirits, unfurl your wings,
In winds of change, the freedom sings.

Together we rise, through dusk and dawn,
With every challenge, new hope drawn.
The heights may strive to test our will,
But in our hearts, the fire will thrill.

So fear not the shadows, fear not the climb,
For in the struggle, we find our rhyme.
With dreams in hand and spirits high,
We'll touch the stars, just you and I.

Fearless Rise

In the dawn's embrace, we stand so tall,
Fearing not the shadows, we break the fall.
With every heartbeat, we claim our might,
Together we rise, igniting the night.

No chains can bind us, no walls can hold,
In the fire of passion, our dreams unfold.
Embracing the journey, we march ahead,
With courage as our guide, no tears to shed.

Through trials and storms, we find our way,
Unfaltering spirits, come what may.
With each brave step, we shatter fears,
A chorus of voices, echoing cheers.

So let the world see, let it ignite,
Fearless we rise, into the light.
With hearts intertwined, our hopes align,
Together we soar, like stars that shine.

In unity, strength becomes our song,
Fearless we stand, where we belong.
With eyes on the horizon, we chase the sun,
In this fearless rise, we are all as one.

Illuminate Your Way

In the depths of night, stars gently gleam,
Whispers of hope, like a soft dream.
When shadows linger, let your heart sway,
Lighting the path, illuminate your way.

With every heartbeat, let courage unfurl,
Shining like gems in this vast, dark swirl.
Breathe in the wisdom that time may cast,
A guiding light through the shadows vast.

Hold fast to your dreams, let them take flight,
Chasing the dawn, igniting the night.
In every heartbeat, let your spirit play,
For in your hands lies the spark to stay.

Embrace the journey, let fears subside,
With love as your compass, you shall abide.
Through valleys of doubt, in shadows of gray,
Remember always, illuminate your way.

So dance with the dawn, and sing to the skies,
Trust in your heart, let it be your guide.
For every flicker, every gentle sway,
Brings forth a light that will never betray.

Beyond the Clouds

High above the world, where dreams take flight,
Above the gray skies, beyond the night.
Winds of change whisper, soft as a sigh,
Leading us onward, to soar and fly.

In the vast unknown, we dare to roam,
Finding our haven, discovering home.
With hearts wide open, embracing the sun,
We dance through the heavens, we become one.

Through trials we rise, like the phoenix so bold,
In the tapestry of life, our stories unfold.
With each breath we take, we claim our space,
Beyond the clouds, we find our grace.

Together we wander, hand in hand,
Through fields of starlight, our hearts expand.
With laughter and love, we light the way,
Guided by hope, come what may.

So look to the stars, let your spirit soar,
Beyond the clouds, there's so much more.
In unity we flourish, together we thrive,
In this endless journey, we're truly alive.

The Courageous Heart

In the silence deep, a heartbeat resounds,
A courage that whispers, where strength abounds.
Through trials and storms, let hope take flight,
With a courageous heart, embrace the fight.

Every step forward, though heavy the weight,
With fire inside, we can't hesitate.
The path may be rugged, the road steep and long,
But together we stand, forever strong.

With dreams as our anchors, we refuse to yield,
In the face of doubt, we wield our shield.
With passion ignited, we forge ahead,
On the wings of courage, fear lies dead.

So rally your spirit, let courage sing,
In the depths of struggle, find the strength to bring.
A symphony of hope, a chorus we start,
In every soul's journey, lies the courageous heart.

With eyes on the horizon, we chase the dawn,
In unity and love, our fears are gone.
Embrace every challenge, let the truth impart,
For in every heartbeat, beats a courageous heart.

Horizons of Promise

Across the sky, colors blend,
New dawn awakens, dreams ascend.
Mountains stand, shadows tall,
Whispers of future, beckoning call.

Seeds of hope in fertile ground,
In every heart, a spark is found.
With every breath, we rise anew,
Horizons gleam, possibilities in view.

Faint stars twinkle in the night,
Guiding souls towards the light.
Together we journey, hand in hand,
In the land of promise, we choose to stand.

Through valleys deep, and rivers wide,
We carry dreams, our hearts our guide.
With courage fresh, we'll brave the storm,
In unity, we're safe and warm.

Horizons stretch as far as sight,
Each step forward, pure delight.
Boundless realms await our gaze,
In life’s embrace, forever ablaze.

The Dance of Determination

In the rhythm of every beat,
Determination guides our feet.
With passion ignited, spirits soar,
To dance through life, forever more.

Each stumble teaches, every fall,
We rise again, standing tall.
For in the struggle, strength is found,
In the dance of life, we're tightly bound.

With every twirl, we find our way,
Facing fears that lead astray.
But hearts united, we shall thrive,
In the dance, we come alive.

To the rhythm of hopes and dreams,
Life's wild song, bursting at the seams.
With open minds, we take the chance,
In this beautiful, bold dance.

No matter the trials we confront,
We'll sway through shadows, never blunt.
For with our spirits intertwined,
A brighter future we will find.

Crafting Your Legacy

Every choice we make today,
Shapes the path we pave and lay.
In whispers soft, or voices strong,
Our legacy is where we belong.

With bricks of love and stones of grace,
We build a life, a sacred space.
Each act of kindness, small yet grand,
Crafts a legacy, hand in hand.

Through trials faced, and joy expressed,
In the depth of struggle, we are blessed.
For every challenge, we embrace,
Is a chance to leave a trace.

Memories woven, threads of gold,
In stories shared, our truth is told.
From every heart, a piece will show,
In the legacy, we choose to grow.

With time as a canvas, we paint our name,
In the tapestry of life, we stake our claim.
Crafting tales that gently weave,
A legacy that we believe.

The Journey Ahead

With every dawn, new paths unfold,
Adventures await, vibrant and bold.
Through misty valleys and peaks so high,
We chase our dreams beneath the sky.

Each step we take, a story told,
In the journey ahead, we are consoled.
With courage our compass, hearts aglow,
We embrace the unknown, let our spirits flow.

Together we wander, side by side,
In moments shared, our spirits glide.
Through storms and sunshine, we remain,
In the journey ahead, love will sustain.

Every twist and turn enriches the soul,
In laughter and tears, we become whole.
With dreams as our map, our hearts as guide,
We step into life with arms open wide.

In unity, we rise and thrive,
In this journey ahead, we come alive.
With each new day, we dare to tread,
Embracing the magic in what lies ahead.

The Gift of Grit

In shadows deep, we find our strength,
With each small step, we go the length.
Through trials fierce, a fire ignites,
Grit guides us on through darkest nights.

A whisper soft, but oh so grand,
It builds us up, it makes us stand.
With every fall, we rise anew,
The gift of grit, forever true.

In countless ways, it shapes our tale,
Through every storm, we shall not pale.
With hearts ablaze, we face the fight,
Grit leads us forth, into the light.

So when the road is rough and steep,
Remember well, the promises we keep.
For in our souls, the spark persist,
The gift of grit is too hard to resist.

Rise Like the Dawn

When darkness falls, and shadows creep,
We find the strength, no time to weep.
With hopeful hearts, we gather round,
And rise again, like the dawn unbound.

The night may chill, but stars will shine,
Guiding us forward, drawing the line.
Each morning brings a brand new start,
A canvas fresh, to paint our art.

Embrace the light that breaks the break,
With every choice, new paths we make.
Together we stand, unyielding and strong,
We rise like the dawn, where we belong.

Through storms and trials, we find our way,
With trust in tomorrow, come what may.
For in our souls, the fire burns bright,
To rise like the dawn, with hope and light.

A Song of Endeavor

In every heart, a song will play,
A melody sweet, guiding our way.
With every step, we voice our dream,
In every note, we find our theme.

With courage bold, we sing aloud,
Against the winds, we stand so proud.
Each verse we write, a tale to tell,
A song of endeavor, we craft so well.

Through highs and lows, the rhythm flows,
In unity, our spirit grows.
Hand in hand, we'll face the night,
Our song of endeavor, a beacon of light.

So let us dance, let voices blend,
In this great journey, there’s no end.
With hearts aglow, we'll chart our course,
A song of endeavor, our greatest force.

The Landscape of Dreams

In the quiet hush, our dreams take flight,
Painting visions, both bold and bright.
Beneath the stars, we dare to roam,
The landscape of dreams, our cherished home.

With every thought, a world unfolds,
A tapestry rich, with stories told.
Through valleys deep and mountains high,
The landscape of dreams, we will not deny.

With hope our compass, we journey far,
Guided by each shimmering star.
In whispered winds, our dreams dance free,
The landscape of dreams, where we shall be.

So let us wander, hand in hand,
Through fields of wonder, a timeless land.
In dreams we trust, our spirits gleam,
Exploring together, the landscape of dreams.

Unbreakable Spirit

In shadows deep, we rise anew,
With strength that's born from trials true.
A heart that beats, a will that fights,
Through darkest days, we find the lights.

With hope as guide, we stand up tall,
Together strong, we'll never fall.
The fire within, it burns so bright,
Our spirit's roar, a fierce delight.

For every wound, a lesson learned,
A brighter flame, within us burned.
With every step, we claim our fate,
A bond unbreakable, it won't wait.

Through storms we sail, through winds we steer,
The path is clear, our path is dear.
With courage vast, we face the night,
Our unbreakable spirit, a shining light.

The Power of Belief

In every dream, a seed is sown,
With faith as roots, our strength has grown.
Through doubts that linger, we stand firm,
Our hearts ignite, the will to affirm.

With whispers soft, the hope will rise,
Our visions vast, beyond the skies.
The universe will bend and sway,
When we believe, we pave the way.

With every thought, we shape our fate,
In every moment, it’s not too late.
The power of belief, a force so strong,
In unity we sing our song.

Embrace the dreams that call your name,
With every spark, we feed the flame.
Together we can shift the tide,
In the power of belief, we take our stride.

Seize the Moment

The clock is ticking, time won’t wait,
Embrace the now, don’t hesitate.
With open hearts, the world we’ll greet,
Each breath a gift, life’s bittersweet.

With every chance, we learn to fly,
In every dream, we touch the sky.
The moments pass, don’t let them slip,
Seize them whole, don’t let them rip.

For in the now, our joys unfold,
The stories told, the tales of old.
With every laugh, with every tear,
Seize the moment, hold it near.

With courage bold, we’ll face the day,
In every choice, we find our way.
The time is now, the world awaits,
Seize the moment, before it fades.

Dance with Destiny

In fate's embrace, we twirl and spin,
With every heartbeat, let love in.
The music plays, our souls in sync,
With every step, we pause and think.

The stars align, the night is ours,
With dreams alight like shining stars.
We'll chase the rhythm, follow the call,
In this grand dance, we'll never fall.

In every turn, the path is clear,
With eyes wide open, we draw near.
Dance with destiny, take a chance,
In life's grand stage, let's learn to dance.

Through joy and pain, we spin around,
With every heartbeat, hear the sound.
A journey shared, a story spun,
Let's dance with destiny, together as one.

Milton Keynes UK
Ingram Content Group UK Ltd.
UKHW020233230824
447326UK00007B/46

9 789916 870389